Debtor's Revenge

How to Be Free of Debt

Michael Walsh

Debtor's Revenge
How to Be Free of Debt
Michael Walsh

Copyright © 2024 Dermot Michael McLaughlin. All rights reserved.
Published by Dermot Michael McLaughlin / Lulu.com
ISBN: 978-1-326-79722-5
Imprint: Lulu.com

The moral and intellectual rights of the copyright holder have been asserted. No part of this publication may be reproduced, distributed, or transmitted in any form or by any means, including photocopying, recording, or other electronic or mechanical methods, without the prior written permission of the copyright holder, except in the case of brief quotations embodied in book reviews and certain other non-commercial uses permitted by copyright law. For permission requests contact the copyright holder at euroman_uk@yahoo.co.uk

Dermot Michael McLaughlin has asserted his right under the Copyright, Designs and Patents Act 1988 to be identified as the author of this work.

Copyright Year: 2024
Copyright Notice: by Dermot Michael McLaughlin. All rights reserved.
The above information forms this copyright notice: © 2024 by Dermot Michael McLaughlin. All rights reserved.

The publisher and author can accept no legal responsibility for any consequences arising from the application of information, advice or instructions in this publication. The information herein is not intended to be construed as legal or professional advice.

BIOGRAPHY

Michael Walsh
The writer whose work spans two centuries.

Michael Walsh is a Liverpool-born Irish author. Said to be Britain's most successful multi-topical author he has so far penned and published more than 70 book titles.

The internationally recognised writer provides articles and columns for numerous magazines and international news media. In 2011 he was awarded 'Writer of the Year' by the publishers of Euro Weekly News. He is a member of the Editorial Board of The Barnes Review and American Free Press.

The successful author re-entered the publishing world as a writer of romantic fiction. **Retribution** was his first successful novel. His experiences as a world-travelling wanderer, whose familiarity with Africa and its violent history he was part of, brought the characters and their darkest deeds to real life.

The success of **Retribution** was enough to inspire the award-winning journalist to pen **The Leaving of Liverpool**. The title is an illustrated autobiographical chronicle of his life and colourful experiences as a British Merchant Navy seaman in the 1950s and 1960s.

During his years at sea, he was to visit over 65 countries. Also, related seafaring books: **Britannic Waives the Rules, Untold Sagas of the Sea Volume I, II, III** and **IV** and **All I Ask is a Tall Ship.**

Michael turned his writing talents to penning **The Stigma Enigma**, the second of his city-vigilante thrillers. The storyline uses many of the penman's page-turning tricks that made **Retribution** a runaway success. **The Soul Mates** is his fourth Merseyside theme book title; a head-swimming mix of the supernatural and the love that dare not speak its name.

Destined to be a best-seller with film and television potential, **The Dovetails Hotel** is a tender and expressive romantic story of Gareth and his ménage a trois lifestyle with two lady owners of **The Dovetails Hotel**.

The entertaining and engaging interludes are accompanied by risqué humour and naughty incidents. A reader writes, 'I thoroughly enjoyed it. I am feeling rather hot.'

Aware of the trailblazing potential of **The Dovetails Hotel** the new genre novelist wasted no time in putting pen to paper. The result was **The Enigma of Tiffany**. Buoyed by his success and the need to meet increasing demand for his gripping style as a storyteller he has now published **The Phantom of Ophelia**.

Michael Walsh's collection of over 1000 inspiring, heart-warming and undoubtedly entertaining poems enjoys global acclaim.

Praise for his literary adventurous 'in touch with the people' pen has been unstinting from Ken Dodd, Bernard Cooper (Guild of Master Craftsmen); Archbishop of Liverpool, Rt. Hon. John Prescott, MP, The Bluecoat Press, Merseyside Police, Radio Port Phillip (Australia) Roger Phillips and Pauline Daniels, BBC Radio Merseyside, Liverpool Daily Post plus various publishers and media editors. Robert Burns (founder of Irish theme pubs); Radio Personality Frankie O'Connor, Willy Russell, playwright: (Shirley Valentine, Blood Brothers).

DEDICATIONS

DEBTOR'S REVENGE is dedicated to my dear wife. I pay patriarchal tribute to our sons. A free thinker, my rebellious independence has not endeared me to all. No regrets, I am what I am; my own man and unburdened by the shackles of convention. Amen!

CONTENTS

- Chapter 1 You are the Victim
- Chapter 2 Credit explained
- Chapter 3 It is not your fault
- Chapter 4 Come Clean
- Chapter 5 The Courts
- Chapter 6 Putting your affairs in order
- Chapter 7 Second Mortgages
- Chapter 8 Eviction
- Chapter 9 If court action is taken against you
- Chapter 10 Credit Rating
- Chapter 11 Dealing with creditors
- Chapter 12 Harassment
- Chapter 13 Notes on Council Tax
- Chapter 14 Bankruptcy or a New Start in Life
- Chapter 15 Who you Owed Money To
- Chapter 16 The Effect on Others
- Chapter 17 Take a Deep Breath
- Chapter 18 Freedom

CHAPTER 1
You are the Victim

The great only appear great because we are on our knees. Let us rise.' - James Larkin.

'Most people made bankrupt each year are honest, ordinary businessmen and women, with fewer than one in ten bankrupted through dishonest dealing.' - Financial Mail on Sunday. July 11 1999.

DAILY MAIL: 43,365 businesses went bankrupt in 1999. (Daily Mail, 4 January 2000) and two million County Court Judgements were registered. Few people have been fortunate enough to avoid falling into financial difficulty. These astounding figures in 2024/2025 are soaring.

This is especially true of the business community where risk is essential to entrepreneurial initiative. It isn't improving and things are worsening:

The number of insolvent companies in England and Wales rose to 4,320 in the second quarter of 2019, the highest in more than five years, from 4,212 in the previous period.

Bankruptcies in the UK show 363,735 collapsed companies from 1975 until 2019 reaching an all-time high of 6,919 companies in the fourth quarter of 2008 and a record low of 924 companies in the second quarter of 1979.

Debt is distressing. Debt negatively affects entire families and communities; Debt is cholesterol in the blood of the economy.

Surprisingly, little is known or even taught about how to avoid debt. This is not an oversight, it is deliberate. Why? Because those operating the banks, the financial markets and debt recovery interests do not want people to know otherwise they would go out of business.

The political ruling class is notorious for investing and ring fencing the banking houses are protecting their investments by voting against the interests of their electors.

Most people in their innocence are lambs to the speculator's abattoirs of greed. Right through and from school financial services, money management and basic business skills should be taught and tested.

The innocent families and owners of small businesses are ambushed by a system as bent as £2 note. The victims have little chance against financial parasites. Many who fall on hard times find themselves worse off when they could and should be better off.

From that moment on theirs is an unending nightmare of intimidating letters, threats and nasty phone calls from people who seem to have an instinct for calling just as visitors arrive.

In times of financial hardship, you are stripped of your dignity and your human and civil rights evaporate. You are vulnerable. The heartless strangers at the door may want your home, your possessions and certainly your last vestige of self-respect.

You feel publicly humiliated. Behind each abusive letter, phone call or debt collector knocking at the door stands the spectre of presiding counsel who holds power over your business and your livelihood.

Under threat is your job, your home and its contents. The system even has the power to deprive you of your liberty. Not surprisingly it is a thoroughly frightening and bewildering experience for you and your family.

I know all about your pain because I have been through it. Through circumstance and through no fault of my own I fell on hard times.

What happened to me happens to many thousands of other unfortunates By learning how to turn the tables I emerged at the other side a stronger, wiser and richer man.

My only regret is that at the time I didn't have a friend who had endured and survived a similar experience. Someone who could explain the unknown to me, take my side and take my hand. A person who could lead me safely to security.

There are plenty of such people around. But being penniless, bankrupt or facing bankruptcy, repossession and humiliations of penury are not something you broadcast. I now do so through ***Debtor's Revenge, How to Be Free of Debt.***

My reasons for doing so are twofold: All my life I have benefited from the experiences of other good-hearted people. Then there is the satisfaction resulting from passing on the benefits of my experience to unfortunates who face similar difficulties. In Debtor's Revenge, you will find that someone who takes away the fear, the threat and humiliation, and returns your pride and self-respect.

Debtor's Revenge was first published in 2008. It is best to assume the content to be unchanged. There may be services or addresses that have changed as addresses can and do change overnight. Once you have the idea simply use Google and follow the dots to the updated information ~ Michael Walsh.

Perseverance

When things go wrong as they sometimes will,
When the road you're trudging seems all up hill,
When the funds are low and the debts are high,
And you want to sigh, but you have to sigh,
When care is pressing you down a bit –
Rest if you must but don't you quit.

Life is queer with its twists and turns,
As every one of us sometimes learns,
And many a fellow turn about,
When he might have won if he'd stuck it out.
Don't give up though the pace seems slow –
You may succeed with another blow.

Often the goal is nearer than,
It seems to a faint and faltering man.
Often the struggler has given up,
When he might have captured the victor's cup;
And he learned too late when the night came down,
How close he was to the golden crown.

Success is failure turned inside out,
The silver tint of the clouds of doubt;
And you never can tell how close you are,
It may be near when it seems afar:
So, stick to the fight when you're hardest hit,
It's when things seem worse that you mustn't quit.

Author unknown

Chapter 2
Credit Explained

'Those who worked were looked upon with contempt and subjected to every possible indignity. Nearly everything they produced was taken away from them and enjoyed by the people who did nothing.

And then the workers bowed down and grovelled before those who had robbed them (tax) of their labour and were childishly grateful to them for leaving anything at all '– Robert Tressell. The ragged Trouser Philosopher (1910).

These days everything is on credit. The average family uses their CREDIT cards for 80% of their purchases: Most of our car and travel costs, the weekly supermarket shop, holidays, hotels, the clothes we buy, dining out, paying bills, and impulse buys. Try to use cash instead.

On average, a small family run shop in your town forfeits £438 pound every MONTH on bank charges levied by the bank debit and credit card charges. By paying in cash, you and your local shopkeeper keeps the money in your community.

Large stores because they have negotiated ultra-low rates denied to their smaller family-owned rivals don't want you to use cash. They want you to use the credit cards.

A famous name American department store makes more money out of the interest they charge on in-house credit card transactions than they do out of the goods they sell. This interest can be as high as 30% with more added on for defaulters.

So, the department stores make 25% on the jumper they sell. The store makes another 30% on their in-house credit card with which you purchase their goods. A nice little earner as Del Boy might say.

The same can be said of holidays. They want you to borrow the money to pay for it. Get your holiday on credit and you're still paying for it long after the memories and photographs have faded.

Then there are home improvements, double-glazing, conservatories, bathrooms, flooring and loft conversions all of which can be paid for on credit.

'I'm more interested in the return of my money than the return on my money.' (Mark Twain)

Credit is Debt and Debt is Usury

Credit card debt like alcohol has its good side but it claims many victims too. Our forefathers were well aware of the dangers posed by moneylenders and their victims.

For hundreds of years, moneylending was outlawed. Oliver Cromwell repealed the laws on usury which enabled him to borrow the money from the banks that was needed to fund his armies.

These days however we can't turn the page of a newspaper or walk down the street without someone pleading with us to take credit offered. Moneylenders make their money from the interest on the money they lend you.

Don't fool yourself that you bought your home for £150,000. You might have done so if you had placed £150,000 in hard cash on the counter or you exchanged a similarly valued property when you made your purchase. Chances are you have a mortgage.

If you took out a £150,000 loan on a mortgage at 4.8% interest over 25 years you will pay in total £257,000. If the interest rate is 8.8% you will cough up £371,000. Respectively, £107,000 or £221,000 more than you borrowed. Until the last penny is paid, the house is not yours but belongs to the bank.

'The best way to rob a bank is to own one.' ~ Bill Moyers. Former U.S. Director of the Institute for Fraud Prevention.'

Cash is Trash

I once attended a sales training seminar provided by one of Britain's largest home improvement companies.

During the training session in which financing of the home improvement was discussed, the salesmen were required to shout, 'CASH IS TRASH' whenever the word cash was used. When the word 'finance' was mentioned all had to shout, 'FINANCE IS FUN!'

The company's sales personnel had their commission reduced by 2% if they failed to get their customers to use the credit option and customers instead arranged cash payment. In other words, this scheme was a stitch-up conspired in by the company and their bank.

Home improvement companies get a bung off the banks for finance deals they arrange to pay for home improvements. Purchasers of the company's home improvement service are enticed to borrow much more than is needed for their home improvement.

For instance: If the client has outstanding debts on their car, the outlay for their holiday and other outstanding debts, they were encouraged to consolidate these outstanding arrears into one debt.

If successfully persuaded, they might end up borrowing £25,000 plus eye-watering interest for their already overpriced £6,000 home improvement.

Chapter 3
It is Not your Fault

Poverty exists not because we cannot feed the poor but because we cannot satisfy the appetites of the rich.

If you are a victim of usury, it is not a failure of yours. It is a win-win success of the corrupt system that the economies of the Western democracies are based on.

In 1933, Germany banned usury. World War II was the consequence of their opting out of the debt system. The same might be said of the Russian Federation, People's Republic of China, Iraq Libya and other countries; these nations opted for economic independence and paid the price in sanctions by the Western Alliance which is run by the banking cartels.

In countries where usury is illegal or under tighter control by governments of integrity none of the hardships endured by the debtors exists.

Bank Interest adds 40 per cent to Everything purchased

Every time you purchase a train ticket; buy a pair of shoes or use public services roughly 40% of your expenditure will go into the vaults of international banking houses.

According to Ellen Brown, chairman of America's Public Banking Institute, a public banking sector would discount up to 40% of everything we buy or use. This is the reason why privately owned banking houses cannot challenge some nationalised banks like those of Russia, China and Iran.

Farmers, manufacturers and transportation costs are dependent upon bank loans. Each supplier in the supply chain from farm and factory to end user must invest, use premises, engage labour, materials and transport, etc. This is before the end product is available. This credit is accumulative and variable.

German Professor Margrit Kennedy reveals that 35% to 40% of everything we buy goes on bank interest. Each time local government and ordinary purchasers spend €100, 40% of the cost is siphoned off by the banking houses accumulative interest rates.

Dr Kennedy discovered that even in today's fiscally prudent Germany bank interest adds 12% to the cost of refuse collection.

When we receive a water bill presume an eye-watering 38% of the invoice value will go directly to the e-vaults of the private banking sector. Britain's largest water authority - London is facing bankruptcy because it cannot afford to meet the interest loans on bank loans. You, the taxpayer will bail the water corporation and the banks out In Germany, a breath-taking 77% of rentable public housing goes into the bank interest.

American citizens need not smirk; compound interest on most mortgages amounts to 80% of what they pay for home or business premises. The home of the free is the home of the free ride if you are an investment banker bondholder, banker or financier.

The noted German researcher and analyst draws heavily on the findings of economist Helmut Creutz. His findings are based on the German economic model. However, if you are not German don't get too excited; the same fraudulent banking system is in place throughout the European Union and the United Kingdom.

Financial sector profits comprise an incredible 40% of the price of whatever Americans purchase. This may go some way to explaining why 1% of Americans own 42% of the national wealth. Only 5% of America's wealth is shared between those making up 80% of the population.

If we had a financial system that transferred private bank interest back to the public purse 35% could be lopped off the price of everything we buy. That means we could buy three items for the price of two; our salaries would go 50% farther than they go today.

Iceland President Ólafur Ragnar Grímsson says, the government bailed out the people and imprisoned the banksters, the opposite of what America and the rest of Europe did.'

It is the Crooked System not a Personal Failure

Few of us set out with the intention of getting into financial trouble and most who do see it as a personal failure. This is far from being the case so don't feel that you are a loser. You are not. You are a victim of system-sanctified corruption.

Most people fall on hard times because of unforeseen circumstances. Often, events outside our control conspire to upset the financial apple cart. There is nothing you can do about inflation which is caused by the government spending too much on the wrong things.

You take out a mortgage but you can't foresee your employer's bankruptcy resulting in your redundancy. You cannot predict illness that negatively affects family income.

Orders may drop so overtime and bonuses are cut. Your spouse might lose what was presumed to be a secure career. Financial institutions benefit from your getting into financial difficulties. They are in a win-win situation.

Very few people become credit risks through bad money management. Not that this makes much of a difference if you're under pressure. If it helps to take away some of the blame game resting unfairly on your shoulders then it does matter.

Stop feeling guilty about the turn of events. Most of the guilt rests on those who driven by greed also gambled on your future ability to pay or/and perhaps loaded the interest so much that their excessive greed brought you to your knees.

Nobody thinks badly of You

Now you have decided to resolve your problems you may be put off by having to bare your soul to strangers. Let me put your mind at rest.

I too ignored the final demands. I let the mortgage slip for several months. I too hoped that something would turn up. I shunned the various agencies that could offer assistance. We all do and that is mistake number one. It is the most expensive mistake of all.

Seek Professional Help

There is no shortage of very nice and genuinely caring people waiting to help you. You will find the Citizens Advice Bureau and Age Concern listed under COUNSELLING AND ADVICE in the Yellow Pages. If they cannot help you, they will tell you who is better able to help you.

Also, check out Yellow Pages INFORMATION SERVICES. Here you will find several agencies paid for or subsidised by various government or European agencies. Believe me, they want to be approached and they genuinely want to help you. It is what they are paid to do.

Don't worry if on occasion you find yourself in front of the wrong desk to deal with your particular problem.

If the agency you have called upon cannot help you, they invariably know someone who can. Their advice is invaluable and you can't put a price on the relief of sharing your burden with someone neutral who understands, is sympathetic, non-judgemental and friendly.

When I finally grasped the nettle and contacted the lenders and the advisory agencies, the court staff, financial professionals and the bureaucrats, I found nothing but friendliness, respect and helpfulness. I cursed myself for not having done so sooner. Catch a Cab: my first port of call was the Citizens Advice Bureau (CAB).

Because of the business complexity of my situation, I opted for my city's large central office rather than a local one.

Volunteers who are fine with domestic concerns usually manage smaller part-time suburban offices. However, they are often out of their depth when faced with the intricacies of small business, commercial or cataclysmic financial failure.

The larger central offices will usually see you briefly when you call or drop in. Having taken your details from you an appointment will be made for you to see a professional who specialises in your particular problems. In my case, I was helped enormously by two talented university students whose hearts were set on graduating as solicitors.

You won't get any bills as CAB is a free service. Of course, when you get back on your feet you may wish to show a little gratitude.

On my first visit, I took with me a folder full of final demands, overdue bills, nasty threatening letters, and a roughly written record of my income and expenditure.

It took courage as I didn't relish the thought of sharing a waiting room with 'other losers' like me. I cringed at the thought of talking about my difficulties to a total stranger. Besides, I wasn't too keen on my flaws being overheard or discussed perhaps by others. This was ignorance on my part.

The small waiting room was warm and well away from the gaze of passers-by. There were plenty of advisory leaflets to read if I wished to remain reserved from the other solitary visitors sharing the waiting room.

After just a few minutes a very pleasant advisor invited me into a small private office. Being past middle-aged, I didn't relish the thought of confessing my sins to such a young person.

In fairness, she was friendly, sympathetic, understanding and professional and most importantly she was non-judgemental. I imagine she had probably heard it all before many times. I felt very much at ease whilst getting my nightmare off my chest I was giving her a brief account of my situation.

The aim was simply to identify the problem and to place my difficulties with someone with the professional expertise to deal with that area of need. There was during our chat a summary of my financial and domestic situation.

After leaving me for a few minutes she returned with a professional debt advisor well used to dealing with situations like mine. As we talked, I felt the burden of guilt and helplessness and disgrace lifting from my shoulders.

I cannot begin to describe the relief as I unburdened myself to someone professional, detached, empathetic and friendly. My problems once shared soon evaporated as talking together we set out on paper the true state of my affairs.

There was my income such as it was and how I saw it developing in the future. Then there was the list of creditors; those I owed money to.

There was then the essential separation of the essential from the less so pressing. My assistant was helping me with that all-important 'all cards on the table' conversation so the big picture could be better seen.

Do it Now

Deal with the problem NOW. The longer you leave it the worse it gets. If you were out of your depth, you wouldn't start swimming further from the shore, would you?

Face up to your situation and resolve to do something about it. Grasp the nettle. It doesn't hurt as much as you think it will. There is a wonderful system in place that will help you get back on your feet.

Chapter 4
Come Clean

You can't begin to put something right until you face up to the fact that it is broken. Don't worry about it making things worse. It doesn't. It makes things better right away. Contact your creditors to let them know your situation.

You Will Not be Going to Prison

Don't panic. You will not be going to prison. The days are long gone when folk were sent to prison for non-payment of debts.

The only people imprisoned for non-payment of debts are those few who can pay something no matter how small and reasonable towards say a court fine and after many court appearances point blank refuse to do so.

The fact is, the prisons are so full of real criminals that the overstretched system simply doesn't have the cells to cope with debtors.

Today, thousands of real criminals are released early simply because the government hasn't the space and has spent the money for more places elsewhere so they're not going to jail you for being unable to pay your bills.

Never Borrow Money to Pay off your Debts

Have you ever tried getting out of a hole by making it bigger? It doesn't work. You end up in a bottomless pit. Don't even think about it. Don't gamble. As one wit observed, the bookie has more paying in windows than paying out ones.

Your Home

Home ownership whilst still under a mortgage is an illusion. In effect, the householder is renting the mortgagee's property which he borrowed from. Home ownership is not popular in mainland Europe where most people rent.

However, losing your home can be avoided in most cases. If it cannot be avoided then it isn't the end of the world. There was a time when you didn't have a home and you did not have a mortgage. Halcyon days! Were you any less a person then?

Homeownership is not the status symbol or the 'bricks and mortar' security investment it once was for your parents and grandparents. There is a very strong financial and mobility argument in favour of rented property. Buying a home is like owning a ship which cannot leave port.

Many sell their homes and move into rented property. Those who do not sell their homes eventually reach a point in their lives where they are no longer able to help themselves. The system will then put them into a residential home and sell their home to cover the costs of keeping them. So much for a life of paying taxes and social security payments.

You will also find that local authorities and housing associations offer property to let, in my part of the world anyway. It is a tenant's market. Many agencies again will provide financial and other assistance. Take it. We are talking about your rights, not their charity.

I know plenty of successful financially secure people who live in what used to be termed council houses. They feel sorry for those crippled by the mortgage ball and chain.

My brother's family lived in a delightful cul-de-sac with lovely neighbours most of whom had nice cars. Their homes were double-glazed by the local authority.

Beautiful new doors were fitted even though there was nothing wrong with the old doors. On the other hand, being a self-employed businessman, I couldn't afford either new doors or windows for my own home.

Did I say my own home? Rubbish! 'My' home was owned by the building society. If I had any illusions at all I was quickly brought back to reality when I fell behind with my mortgage. Local authority or Abbey National, is there a difference? Yes! The former is much more flexible and less likely to evict you.

Walk softly but carry a Big Stick

Much of the debt recovery system is based on empty threats and bluster. Understand it and you won't fear it.

Of course, some will imply dire consequences should you fail to meet your commitments. It has to be bluster because you are well protected and Teflon coated by law.

Never allow yourself to be frightened or intimidated by letters, personal phone calls or visits. Write or state your case coolly and professionally. Don't give in to persistence. You are in control.

You end the letter when you have forcefully made your point; likewise, you place the phone in its cradle or close the door when you have stated your case. There is no point in repeating it.

Answer All Correspondence and Keep Copies

Keep all debt-related correspondence: letters from building society, credit card and financial institutions, etc. Keep copies of your return correspondence. Try to avoid making promises you cannot keep. It doesn't help you or them.

Prioritise Debts

The first thing you do when setting out on a journey is take out a map to give you a clear picture of your undertaking.

You do not have to be an accountant or an entrepreneur to set out in writing your situation. List separately your assets and your liabilities. By doing so you provide a clear at at-a-glance figure of your true situation.

Chapter 5
The Courts

If you receive court papers fill them in or get someone to help you; a relative or close friend. Most towns and cities have local legal aid solicitors' practices happy to advise or help you. Likewise, a local Citizens Advice Bureau (Yellow Pages COUNSELLING AND ADVICE) and Age Concern. Also, check out Yellow Pages INFORMATION SERVICES.

Let us begin by assessing your situation. Don't exclude your family; they will be very supportive, and sympathetic. Of course, several brains work better than one. They have an interest in your survival too.

The first thing you need to do is put down on paper your financial situation as it is and not as you would like it to be. We call this your FINANCIAL STATEMENT. It is essential so let us get on with it.

FINANCIAL STATEMENT (MONTHLY) INCOME

WAGES	FAMILY
Your Wages	Child Support
Wife or Partner's Wages	Maintenance
Other Income	Other
Lodger	

STATE BENEFITS OTHER INCOME

Income Support
Family Credit
Pension
Child Benefits
Other Benefits

NOTES:

Note 1: Do not include overtime payments or bonuses unless in the unlikely event they are guaranteed and consistent.

Note 2: Benefits include Child Benefit (family allowance).

Note 3: Include any payments made by residents such as parents or children who may be contributing to your bills.

Note 4: You can and should put down outgoings such as trips to the cinema, travel fares (shopping, family visits) other than work-related, some socialising, alcohol and cigarettes. As long as they are not excessive, they are regarded as legitimate expenses.

Note 5: Remember to list car expenses; work tools, fuel, servicing and repairs, MOT and insurance.

Note 6: Nobody is going to argue with you if you put down £10 per person per week for clothing. Don't forget school uniforms or work wear.

Total Family Income

Financial Statement Expenditure

LIVING COSTS

Mortgage
Prescriptions
Ground rent
Repeat/Replacement Medicines
Home Insurance
Laundry
Life Insurance
Endowment
Telephone Bills
Service Charges
Council Tax
Child Care Costs
Day/Nursery Care

HOUSEKEEPING

Food, sanitary needs, nappies household necessities, special needs requirements, TV, household items, school meals.

TRAVEL COSTS

Bus/Train Fares: Children
Clothing for Children, dependants and self
Car Tax
Spouse/Partner
Monthly Petrol
Children
Car Insurance
Car Maintenance
Maintenance/Child Support
Fuel
Electricity
Fines
Gas
Other
TV Licence

TOTAL MONTHLY INCOME _____

TOTAL MONTHLY EXPENDITURE _____

MONEY LEFT OVER FOR CREDITORS _____

NOTES:

Before you complete your FINANCIAL STATEMENT photocopy so that you have spares for the future should they need up dating.

When you have completed your FINANCIAL STATEMENT each of your creditors will need to see a copy. You will also need to bring a copy if you are appearing at a court or mediation panel.

It is an important document; your survival plan if you like. Look after it and it will serve you well.

Chapter 6
Putting Your Affairs in Order

Priority debts are those that will if they remain unpaid threaten your home (repossession), your liberty (imprisonment), or your basic needs (food, heat, communication).

Here then is a list of such debts followed by the possible consequences, which are not the same as probable consequences.

Priority and Possible Consequences

Mortgage Arrears — Repossession of your home
Rent Arrears — "   "
Second Mortgage — "   "
Secured Loans — "   "
Council/Community Tax — Bailiff Action/Imprisonment
Charge Arrears — "   "
Water Rates Arrears — Water Supplies Cut Off
Gas/Electricity Arrears — Supplies Cut Off
Unpaid Fines — Imprisonment
Maintenance Child Support Arrears — Imprisonment
Tax Arrears — Bailiffs/Imprisonment
Telephone — Disconnection

Help is at Hand

All other debts such as credit cards, hire purchases, unsecured loans, and overdrafts are relatively unimportant. They are non-priority.

Because you are not the first to fall behind with payments each of the above has a safety net to catch you, to stop you falling further and to help you get back on to your feet again. because of shared interests, your creditors want to be kept informed of your situation and they do want to help you.

If you follow this advice then most of the consequences listed above will be avoided. Nobody wants your home other than you. Nobody, not even the Inland Revenue wants to put you in prison. None of the utilities wishes to deprive you of their services and nobody wants to send in the bailiffs. All these things can be avoided but you have to help the helpers to help you.

Mortgage

When plunder becomes a way of life for a group of men in society, over time they create for themselves a legal system that authorises it and a moral code that glorifies it' – Frederic Bastiat, French economist.

Knowing that we treat the mortgage as a priority the mortgage providers are pretty quick to sense trouble.

It won't be long before letters expressing their concern arrive. At about three missed payments you will receive a request that you call and discuss the matter so do so.

Contact your building society by letter or telephone. Simply explain that you are having difficulty in maintaining your repayments. Mention the reason why you face difficulties and explain that you would like to see an advisor. At this stage, you are probably behind with your payments anyway so you're only stating the obvious.

Advisors don't bite. Keep your appointment, remember to take a copy of your Financial Statement with you.

If you are already taking advice such as from CAB (Citizens Advice Bureau) or AGE CONCERN you will be better thought of. It shows you are taking professional advice and are dealing with your problems responsibly.

You will not be criticised or humiliated. The only person who knows the purpose of your visit is the adviser. They will look at your situation as they have looked at many others as you are not the first. Using their experience, they will suggest ways by which the situation can be resolved.

They have many options open to them. They can even re-schedule your mortgage. This means reducing the payments and extending the payback period.

Usually, this will be over the coming 12/24-month period but it can be stretched to the end of your mortgage. They can put your mortgage payments on hold or reduce them for a temporary period until you are back on your feet.

If you and your partner work less than sixteen hours a week you may be eligible for Income Support which includes help with your mortgage interest payments.

The DSS (Benefits Agency) would make these payments directly to your lender. Check it out. Such people are there to get you through a troubled period. Take advantage of them.

If your home is worth less than the mortgage, and many are for a variety of good and bad reasons, tell your lender. They will take this into account when looking at options. They don't want to sell a house for £150,000 against a mortgage of £165,000 even if you are ultimately responsible for the shortfall.

Mortgage Time Scales

Three Months: Letters expressing concern and inviting you to contact them.

Six Months: It is now regarded as serious. A visit to your local branch is now essential. Make an appointment with an advisor, sit down and explain the situation. They can then help you with advice and possible alternative solutions.

Legal Department and negotiation: Unless something can be resolved such as an arrangement to resume payment plus a little each month off the outstanding payments it is usually passed to the building society's legal department. This will add considerably to your debt. Avoid it if you can.

If you are then dealing directly with their legal experts' negotiations are still open and this period can be used to create delaying tactics. Drag out correspondence and leave replies to the last minute. Ask questions which necessitate a reply. Some of these have to be referred back to the lender for their input.

8/9 Months. If a deal has not been worked out the lender's legal department will then apply to the courts for a repossession order. This takes up more time. It can take up to three months just to get a date for a court hearing and a further three months can elapse before it takes place. You are now nearly fifteen months ahead of the game

When the court hearing date is known it provides further opportunity for delaying tactics. Start negotiating again by perhaps showing that a certain level of payment has been maintained. This may fall short of the arranged monthlies but it is indicative of your taking your commitments seriously and responsibly.

It could and should be that during this period running up to the court hearing the date being known you have managed to disentangle yourself from the financial mess you were in. Keep negotiating. It can't do any harm but can do much good in your favour.

Even if a repossession order is granted the lender is still open to doing a deal so do spin things out and always keep the address and telephone number of the local main office of your CAB to hand. They will always help you through a crisis. They will even call on your tormentors and negotiate on your behalf.

AN IRRESISTIBLE OPTION

Experiencing financial difficulties after we separated my wife kept an appointment with a family solicitor. Bear in mind we had two school-age sons. I couldn't help as out of work and homeless; I was staying with a friend. The solicitor's service was free of charge. It is an entitlement.

My wife and I were facing divorce anyway. My wife was made to understand that if she started the divorce proceedings then being the single mother of children she could not be evicted. Suck it up, mortgage lender. Our family home was secure.

Potential problem. Ours had been a good marriage. At such an early stage of abandonment, my wife was not entitled to a divorce. What now? Much to my disgust and my wife's dilemma it was suggested that she dream up a situation in which divorce like right now was possible.

Her solicitor suggested that she claim I was violent towards her, which I never was. Never in my life have I ever raised my hand to a woman.

That was by-the-by, the pen did its evil work – and my wife's divorce went through immediately. She and my sons from that moment on had a state-paid permanent roof over their heads.

Incidentally, my wife and I stayed friendly and mutually supportive and on the best of terms until her passing on due to cancer of the lungs. For years, I had begged my wife and offered to help her quit smoking. She was deaf to my advice.

You decide which is the most important. A registrar's piece of paper stating the bleeding obvious – that you are mutually committed to each other – or a home for your wife and children?

Some Options

Adding the arrears to the total mortgage debt.

Increasing the payments to repay the arrears over a set period of time; say 12 or 24 months.

For a set period paying off only the interest.

If you have an endowment mortgage you may be able to cash the endowment policy and use the money to pay off the arrears. Take the advice of your advisor on this. They are obliged by law to give you the best possible advice. Failing to do so can lay them open to litigation.

If you can cash your endowment, you might arrange another policy or you could ask the lender to change your mortgage into what is known as a Capital Repayment Mortgage. This makes your payments up with both interest and capital.

Chapter 7
Second Mortgage

Never trip over the same stone twice ~ Roman maxim.

The second mortgage is a loan secured against your home. The loan settles your outstanding mortgage and you start again from scratch.

This means that should you default then the lender could seize your home so that it is sold to raise the money still outstanding. Such lender institutions tend to be less flexible than the building societies. However, they will usually try to accommodate you unless yours is a hopeless case.

A visit or appointment with an adviser is usually arranged. The lady or gentleman will call and see you at your home to discuss options.

Don't be resentful. In my experience, these advisors tend to be just as understanding, sympathetic and helpful as the building society advisors. They are there to listen, to offer sympathy and provide solutions.

WHOA! If you are thinking of taking out a second mortgage your first port of call HAS TO BE your first mortgage lender, presumably the one who mortgaged your home.

If through ignorance you go to a lender other than the one that arranged your home loan you are running double the risk.

Your first lender is cheaper and far more flexible. Only go for a secured loan elsewhere if the first won't back you. That said if this is the case, should you be taking it out at all?

Some Options

Making reduced payments for an agreed period of time.

Increasing payments to recover arrears over a set period of time.

Re-scheduling them so that the outstanding payments are tacked on to the back.

In the unlikely event that any of your creditors, priority or otherwise, refuse your offer to continue to pay what you can afford even if it is only a token payment.
Then if it goes to court this will go very much in your favour. It shows good intent and an ability to meet your commitments even if in a reduced way.

Good Advice

You might have heard of people giving up and handing (or posting) the keys of their abandoned home to their mortgage lenders. Don't do it. It works against you. Never hand the keys back without taking professional advice.
If you do give the keys back you are still responsible for the outstanding mortgage. The lender will put your home up for auction. If it goes for peanuts, they could not care less as you are still responsible for the mouth-watering difference. There is no guarantee that the local authority will house you; least of all in a home that you would find acceptable.
You would still, however, be responsible in law for the mortgage payments until the house is sold. This could take years. Always take advice. The Citizens Advice Bureau is your first call. Even at this desperate stage they will likely be able to offer a solution.

Chapter 8
Eviction

'If we don't guarantee even the most menial of workers a living wage, we are not a free society, we've just changed the mechanics of slavery.' – David Gerrold.

You cannot be evicted without a Court Order and Court orders for Eviction are virtually impossible to gain.

Never be afraid of going to a court if summoned to do so. They are impartial affairs without a jury being present and rarely do they make your situation worse.

These days there is no need to represent yourself as most courts – if you ask, will provide you with a free solicitor.

We live in a world of specialisation. Leave such things to the specialists. See your local advice centre which will arrange for you to be advised and represented by a properly qualified person without charge to you.

The Inland Revenue

The Inland Revenue may appear to have forgotten you and you can be forgiven for thinking out of sight out of mind.

Fool yourself if you will but believe me there is no escape. The taxman knows he is a priority and that he can't be cheated even by death, but oh, yes, he can.

One day, when you are smirking at your apparent success in evading the taxman he will turn up and your life will be laid bare before you.

He will (I am assuming you are self-employed) go through your accounts and when the blood drains from your face he will add the interest. You have got to believe it.

The taxman is single-minded in his pursuit and less flexible than any of the other miscreants when eyeing your hard-earned sobs with a fine-tooth comb.

You won't escape by your being the beneficiary of an 'unfortunate' fine. He would then make an assessment and you would end up paying even more. He will. If he can, the taxman will get blood out of a stone.

Play for time by all means

A factor that does help is the tax collector's misguided belief that you have been salting away 'his' money. Now that the cards are stacked against you, he thinks by one means or another you will make up the shortfall. 'Okay, guvnor; it's a fair cop. I'll come clean.'

Alternatively, he mistakenly believes that as you are something of an entrepreneur you will somehow magic the cash up. Failing that you can make a realistic settlement.

By this, I don't mean offering £10 a month. If you owe the Inland Revenue, say £26,000 then look at perhaps four instalments of £6,500 within the year. Make an unrealistic offer if you like. If nothing else it is a great delaying tactic.

If you can't or won't pay what happens then?

He will petition your bankruptcy.

Sounds dreadful doesn't it

The good news is that the man from Her Majesty's Inland Revenue is so slow-moving he should be in the reptile house off-season.

Lethargic! He invented the word. You walk into your local taxation office and you might occasionally see the lifting of a reptilian eyelid but nothing more.

You could be talking years here. I simply don't know because in the end I gave up waiting for him to deliver and I petitioned for my bankruptcy.

It cost me £370 (in 1999 but it is not as easy now). I was at least in control as far as the timing goes. This is a big advantage.

CAUTION: Do not try to obtain a personal bankruptcy if your income is sufficient to repay your creditors even by the minimum monthly drip. Bankruptcy is an option when and only when there is no possibility of your income or your assets repaying your creditors.

The County Court

County Court appearances and judgements are best avoided. If nothing else they add to your costs and they are a hassle when you least need the hassle.

Fortunately, your creditors have little faith in the court's recovery procedures. Consequently, whatever their threats to the contrary they are as reluctant as you are to use the court system. Often, it is an empty threat.

The courts you may be involved with are not criminal courts as debt is not a criminal offence. There are no juries and no press.

You will not be rubbing shoulders with miscreants or mass murderers. The officials you will deal with will be very similar in appearance and dress to perhaps a school secretary or local businessman or woman.

You will also find that these hearings are held in private so no public gallery, no reporters; often just yourself but why not take a friend? Often but not always there will be the person you owe money to or their representative.

Think of people as a mirror. If you are courteous and pleasant, they will be. If you are arrogant or insolent they will respond in kind.

You will find court officials understanding, helpful and sympathetic unless, of course, you are trying to pull a fast one. Be honest and open and you have absolutely nothing to fear.

The job of the District Judge is rarely to apportion blame. If there was clear evidence of mismanagement or foolishness you may be mildly censured. But nobody is out to make your life difficult.

Officials will lean over backwards to help you resolve your difficulties. The only purpose of these hearings is to resolve a problem as amicably as possible in a way that is financially reasonable for both parties concerned. They are not slanging matches.

Be cool and matter-of-fact. Remain detached, almost as if you are here on behalf of someone else. Draw what conclusions you can but it is usually the debtor (that is you) rather than the creditor (the person you owe money to) who walks out with a smile on their face.

A final point. Always attend. I know that you would rather be anywhere else on earth than be cross-examined on anything as personal as financial hardship. Think of it as being like a visit to the dentist. A little uncomfortable but WOW! What an investment in a pain-free future.

Chapter 9
If Court Action is Taken Against You

As through this world I've wandered, I've seen lots of funny men, some will rob you with a six-gun and some with a fountain pen.' -- Woody Guthrie.

You will receive a default summons that will state precisely what your creditor's claims are. If you contest the claim then do so. It is a great delaying tactic and at this point, I almost feel sorry for the person you owe money to.

Send the attached Form of Reply to the creditor and state any offer of settlement. Enclose a copy of your FINANCIAL STATEMENT. Send a copy of both to the court.

I know a very rich man whose tactic is to use the courts to avoid paying creditors. During the claims process, he employs every delaying mechanism open to him.

He delays by replying that he is going on a pre-booked holiday or business trip. He fakes illness, he disputes claims, and he finds fault with the work that was done.

He does so to a point when his pursuer gives up. He reckons that nine out of ten do so. The last I saw of him he was driving around in a Ferrari. It is unlikely he paid for it.

Invariably your creditor will at this point accept your offer. If he should not then the court will decide on the settlement terms.

It won't be necessary for you to appear at the court; you will be informed in writing. However, should you disagree with the court's proposed settlement terms you can ask for a hearing at which you can state your case.

You must inform the court of your inability to meet the terms proposed with 14 days otherwise you are bound by them. When you appear before the District Judge you can set your stall out for his or her consideration.

Once an order to pay has been made you should, of course, meet your new commitments. If you cannot afford them then pick up Form N245 at any local County Court Office and fill it in. By doing so you may apply for a reduction in the arranged payments.

Advantages of a County Court Judgement

Although your creditors cannot add what they would like to add to the amount owed to them, court costs will be added. These are on a fixed scale, will include solicitor's fees and will be guided by the total amount of money owed.

Being sued through a County Court means that your name will be on the Register of County Court Judgements for six years.

Forget the advice to the contrary. It will not be removed for six years. However, by this time the credit checking agencies are only too well aware of your predicament and so you are a well-marked man or woman anyway.

If you do not make regular payments your creditors (reluctantly) could take further action against you. This could incur extra costs for them too. Consequently, they are most reluctant to do so. If you cannot pay then apply for payments to be reduced.

There is one scam for you to avoid. It will unnecessarily cost you a lot of money. You pay an agency that on your behalf will contest any CCJ claims against you.

While it is being contested (without a chance of success) the County Court Judgements are temporarily removed. Then you go and purchase your car, holiday, home improvement or whatever. After doing so you or your advisors lift the contestation and all the CCJs fall back into place

Not likely! Remember that the credit rating system that will investigate your creditworthiness is not wholly linked to the County Court system. They have their ways of finding out whether you are a good credit risk or not. It is far superior to the court's system.

It is also a myth to believe that the County Court Judgment set against you is lifted if you pay off the debt. It is not lifted so the only advantage of settling the debt prematurely is that that having done so will be recorded on it. It will still stay for six years.

The only way a County Court Judgement is removed is for it to be paid (met) in full within a month of the Judgement being recorded. If it is paid after that period then it will be registered for six years but will have the word 'SATISFIED' attached to it.

Chapter 10
Credit Rating

People tend to think of courts as a last resort because a CCJ (County Court Judgement) may block credit for six years.

Don't concern yourself unduly. If your financial situation has deteriorated to a point where a court order is possible then believe me you are already on 'the shit list'.

Credit ratings these days are right on the button long before the credit risks hit the courts. Most lenders are 'wired up' to centralised credit reference agencies. As soon as you default on any payment, they know about it.

A County Court Judgement, if made against you, would only serve to underline what they already know.

An interesting point is that a person with half a dozen County Court Judgements against him or her but who is settling on the button as required carries a higher credit rating than someone without CCJs but is consistently slipping behind with regular payments.

If you do have CCJs against your name you are perfectly entitled to state your case on the same report as a mitigating circumstance. This gives the people considering any future credit the opportunity to make up their minds about you.

Don't assume that because your credit rating is poor or you have CCJ against you, you will be denied credit.

All lenders have their guidelines and one often differs from another's. There are other factors too: the buoyancy of the market, and how much surplus money they have available to lend. They can tighten up or loosen up by the day.

I was once refused £3,000 credit by a lending house. Coincidentally and almost simultaneously I ordered a credit card which arrived a week or so later that offered me immediate access to a £6,000 credit

On checking the small print, I discovered that the company that had just given me £6,000 owned the financial institution that had refused me £3,000. You work it out. I cannot.

In the last resort, don't worry too much about gaining credit. When you learn how to live (again) and work outside the credit system you inevitably become much richer and free of threat.

In September 2007 I retired and received my meagre state pension. I settled my last debt accrued on my credit card. I immediately cut it in half and dropped it in the bin. Never did I request a replacement.

It can be supposed that during the intervening 18 years I have faced lean times. But I never borrowed a penny – perhaps family helped me out with an interest free loan. I am better off now than I have ever been. I don't owe a brass cent to anyone. I am free.

Have you any idea how much interest you have paid on credit acquired since you left school? Don't work it out or you won't sleep at night.

Just as there are people who don't have television sets in their homes and are better off without them, others get by without credit. Surprise, surprise, they have more money than you and me.

Interestingly, they are not as traceable and accountable either. We do live in a Big Brother system. The Inland Revenue and smaller Big Brothers have cyber connections to the very air you breathe. Deny them as much as you can.

Most of those caught by the Inland Revenue, Customs & Excise (VAT) etc. telling porkies have their collars felt because their lifestyle exceeds their stated income. Tax inspectors will take a close but discreet look at your home, certainly your auto and your lifestyle.

Try convincing them that your £20,000 a year income pays for your £200,000 home, £150,000 car and several holidays of a lifetime each year.

Deal in cash as much as you can. I remember asking a builder friend of mine what he turned over each year. He told me, £200,000. I asked him how much of that was in traceable cheques; about £5,000 he responded.

On the face of it, my builder friend is very well off. On paper, he is at his wit's end. He doesn't spoil it by being too ostentatious about his real wealth. The less they know about you the better it is for you.

Remember the richest institutions in the world are the lending houses and banks. They are obscenely rich because they're milking you so much that you become anorexic. Separate from them and then watch your financial muscle grow. Live outside their usury system. It is their loss, not yours.

Credit Reference Agencies

'The only difference between a tax man and a taxidermist is that the taxidermist leaves the skin.' ~ Mark Twain.

Credit Reference Agencies do not have blacklists. Their purpose is to provide accurate information about your credit record.

It is the person or organisation considering your credit request that will look at it and make a decision. Most lenders have their code that will be based on a points system based on the information you give to them and the information they already have.

The area in which you live will count for or against you, your current financial commitments, age, employment record, prospects, and the type of house you live in, local authority, rented or owned.

Whether you are single, married, or have children; how many dependents? It will all stack up to reach the points required (or not). Thereby hangs the decision.

Lenders are not obliged to tell you why you have been refused credit but may indicate the reason why. You can certainly ask (written) why you were refused.

Their reply will allow you to see if the refusal was justified. If not then ask the lender what procedures are open to you to either challenge it or offer the opportunity to provide a reason why you no longer deserve to be refused.

For instance, people have been refused credit simply because the previous occupant of the house or flat had a bad credit record. In some cases, a credit-worthy son shares the name of his less-than-credit-worthy dad. On the other hand, consider, do you really want or need to be in debt?

Point to Ponder: These days you can be excused for not registering on the electoral roll. Who wants to vote anyway? However, it is important that you be registered as this is a major factor when lenders consider your request.

You have a legal right to know the name of the Credit Reference Agency that the lender asked for details about you. You must do it within 28 days. Simply ask by writing to the lender. They must tell you within seven working days. If they did not ask a credit reference agency then they are not obliged to reply to you.

Your letter will read like this:

Your address:

Dear Car Sales,

I am writing under Section 157 of the Consumer Credit Act, 1974. Please tell me the name of any Credit Reference Agency that has given information about me. I expect a reply within seven days of your receiving this letter.

It isn't necessary for you to be applying for credit to know what information is recorded against you by a Credit Reference Agency. You can write to them and ask for a copy of your file.

YOU NEED TO ~ some of this information may need updating:

Send £1 (not refundable).
Give your full name and address with your postcode.
Give any other addresses you have lived at during the previous six years.

If you have run a business then give its name and address. Separate information may be set against its details.

The agency may ask for further information but is unlikely to do so if you have followed these guidelines. It must either provide you with your file within seven days or tell you that it has no information on you.

Your letter will read like this:

Dear Credit Reference Agency,

I am writing under Section 158 (1) of the Consumer Credit Act 1974. Please send me a copy of my file. I enclose a postal order/cheque for £1.

I have lived at the above address for three years. Before that, I lived at 101 High Street, Our Town, O1 7UR. I expect a reply within seven working days of your receiving this letter.

The four main Credit Reference Agencies are:

CCN Group Ltd, Consumer Affairs Department, PO Box 40, Nottingham, NG7 2SS

Credit and Data Marketing Services, CCA Department, Dove Mill, Dean Church Lane, Bolton, Lancashire, BL3 4ET

Equifax Europe (UK) Ltd, Consumer Affairs Department, 1a North Avenue, Clydebank, Glasgow, G81 2DR

Infolink Ltd, CCA Department, Regency House, 38 Whitworth Street, Manchester, M60 1QH

You can ask that your file be amended if:

The file contains information about other people with whom you have no financial connection.

It contains incorrect information.

Note: Always follow the agency's advisory notes.

Agencies are only allowed to give information about (1) you, (2) people with the same name or a very similar name living at the same address.
(3) Other family members living in your household. (4) Other people sharing your address with whom you have a financial connection.

Agencies must not provide information about other people if (1) they have not lived at the same address as you at the same time or (2) if they have reason to believe that the person has no financial connection with you.

There is other useful information and guidelines relating to credit reference agencies and your possible corrections of file etc.

If you pop into the Citizens Advice Bureau or Trading Standards Office you can pick up a copy of Know Your Rights No.2. Office of Fair Trading;' No Credit' booklet. It is free. It is very useful.

If you have difficulty getting a copy or you feel lazy write to The Director General of Fair Trading, Field House, 15/25 Bream's Buildings, London, EC4A 1PR.

Chapter 11
Dealing with Creditors

The First Essential Letter

Write or type the following letter and send it to each of your creditors. Modify or re-style it to suit the situation but do stick to the essentials. Include the bracketed paragraph only if it is appropriate).

Date
Creditor's Name
Address

Dear Sir / Madam,

I have been experiencing some difficulty in meeting my financial commitments. I have visited my local Citizens Advice Bureau spent some time with their representative and have taken their advice about my financial difficulties.

So that I might budget to arrange offers of repayment to all of my creditors I would be grateful if you would forward to me an up-to-date balance of my account with details of any interest being charged. (I would also appreciate a copy of the original agreement with you).

In the meantime, I hope you can see your way to suspending any legal or other action on my account until offers of repayment can be offered.

I would also appreciate it if you would consider the suspension or reduction of any interest charges. Your cooperation and understanding in this matter are appreciated and I look forward to an early reply.

Yours faithfully, Mr Grateful-Citizen.

The letter will have the effect of letting your creditors know you have hit a bad patch and are no longer able to service your debt as agreed. Fine, that is the real world and they are as much a part of it as you are.

You will find most if not all of your creditors understand. In my case, several credit card lenders immediately froze the interest.

There was no point in them continuing with it and amounts to a considerable saving. All interest would do was increase a debt unlikely to be honoured anyway. They also have a vested interest in avoiding artificially inflated debts.

You will be asked to cut your credit card or debit card in half and return it immediately. That doesn't make matters worse.

If you had already fallen behind with your payments you were unlikely to receive further credit anyway. You would also by now be listed as a bad risk. All you have done is acknowledge the situation so what was the big secret anyway?

You will receive an acknowledgement from your creditors and they will ask you what you intend to pay regularly. The ball is in your court. Pass it back.

From this point on the heat was off. I was on the road to recovery. All I was called upon to do from here on was to pay off the now interest-free debt.

At this stage, I owed the credit card suppliers £20,000 and all of it was now interest-free. I had landed on my feet. Why hadn't I done it years earlier? All that dead money! I could scream.

Date
Creditor's Name,
Address

Dear Sir/Madam,

Creditor's Reference Number

I have now received replies from my creditors and can make offers on repayment. My financial situation which hopefully isn't long-term term is due to (explain your situation; loss of a job, wife's earnings, illness . . ..)

The enclosed financial statement provides details of my total income and essential expenditure. I am making similar offers to my other creditors. Copies are available should you wish to see them.

I have visited the Citizens Advice Bureau and am taking their advice on these matters. Whilst this offer is smaller than that originally agreed I feel that under the circumstances it is realistic.

I will contact you immediately should my circumstances improve and provide you with a revised payment proposal.

To avoid my debt increasing I would be grateful if you would be willing to suspend any interest charges accruing on my debt to yourselves.

I thank you for your understanding and cooperation on this matter. I look forward to your acceptance of my proposal.

Please send me a payment book. I will commence payment on receipt of the same or otherwise immediately I have your acceptance.

Yours faithfully, Mr A. Citizen

I can almost hear you asking

What should you offer and will it be acceptable? It depends on your circumstances. Work it out this way. You have your FINANCIAL STATEMENT in front of you.

You have already set your PRIORITY DEBTS against your TOTAL INCOME. Whatever is left is to be divided evenly among the non-priority debts. Okay, do so.

As a guide, I can tell you that typically I owed £80,000 across four credit cards. In each case, I offered a settlement at £20 per month. Each of the credit card providers accepted my offer. Sometimes I wasn't able to keep my promises. I simply resumed after two or three months.

I know it would take fifty years to repay each £6,000 at the rate of £120 a year. They accept it for two reasons: a bird in the hand is worth two in the bush and the cost of negotiating a higher figure than you are unable to repay isn't worth it.

Might they take you to court to enforce it or increase the amount? Only if according to your FINANCIAL STATEMENT, you are in a position to offer more.

If for instance, you have only £60 a month left over after settling your priority debts and day-to-day needs then the court would be unlikely to try and get blood out of the stone. I don't think it would even get to court.

Do I feel sorry for my credit card creditors? Like hell I do. I am now all too painfully aware of the extent of their greed.

Did they feel sorry for me as I struggled to meet excessive interest payments while my kids went without?

No, they just tried to screw me further. Save your sentiments for those who are truly deserving. I have yet to meet a deserving slave owner.

No money left over

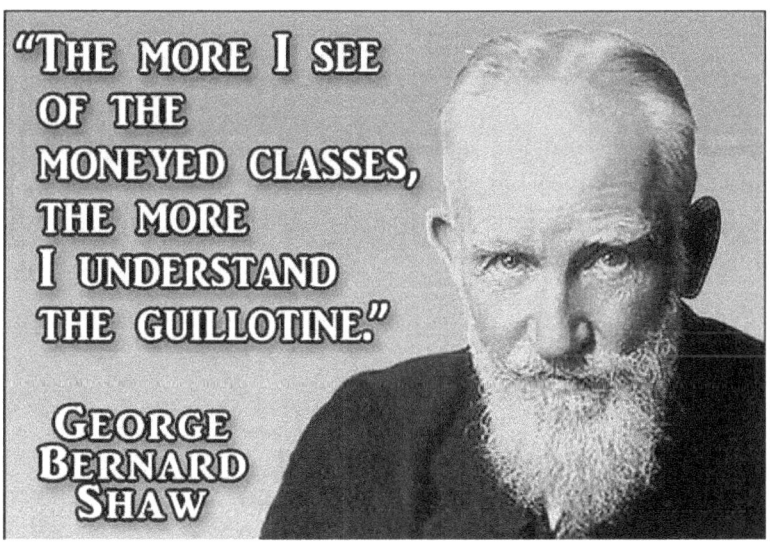

It could be that after working on your FINANCIAL STATEMENT you discover to your horror that you don't have anything at all to spare. Should this be the case then the next letter is I am afraid inevitable:

Date

Creditor's Name,
Address

Account/Creditor's Reference No

Dear Sir / Madam,

I have now received replies from all my creditors. My difficulties as earlier explained are due to (explain difficulties…).

The enclosed financial statement provides details of my total income and essential expenditure. I have visited and taken advice from my local Citizens Advice Bureau and drawn on their self-help booklet provided for those sharing my unfortunate situation.

As you can see, my current income is insufficient to meet agreements with my creditors. I wonder therefore if you would be kind enough to freeze interest and any action on the outstanding amount for three months.

This period should enable me to improve my situation to a point where I can make an offer or resume payments as arranged. Should my circumstances change in the meantime I will, of course, contact you immediately.

I do appreciate that it is a very difficult situation for you and I do apologise. I am simply not in a position to do otherwise. Your understanding and co-operation are appreciated. I hope that our good relations can be maintained.

Yours faithfully,
Mr A. Citizen

What if they do not accept my offer

The response you may get is that the sum offered is too small. This may be true but they cannot have what isn't yours to give. Never allow yourself to be pressured. Stick by your guns because you hold most of the aces.

Remember that when these financial arrangements were set up in the first place you did not have a crystal ball and neither did your suppliers. You took a chance and so did they. You could explain:

If you paid them what they were asking then their upwardly revised amount would need to be taken from another creditor who would pursue it and might make life difficult for you.

You would need to shave essential expenditure further and this you simply cannot do.

If other creditors have accepted your (similar) offer tell them so. This gives a clear indication that it is they who are unreasonable.

It could be that their self-interest demands that you pay less to your priority debts. Don't give in. Explain to them why your priority debts are a priority. You have to maintain an existence of sorts to recover your situation.

You might also point out to them that as soon as you have dealt with your priority debts and stabilise your financial position you will be better placed to increase your offer.

Be prepared to explain why you are spending xxxx amount on whatever.

If your creditor/s will not suspend interest then challenge them to take you to court, implying that you will suspend all payments thus forcing them to take you to court. They know that in law they would not be able to charge interest from the date the judgement was made. You have got them in a corner.

Chapter 12
Harassment

Your creditors are free to remind you from time to time to suggest a revision of arrangements. They are not allowed to harass or pressurise you. It is illegal for them to threaten, abuse, or insult you.

This includes the (empty) threat to put you before a criminal court. Debt is not a criminal offence but claiming that it is to frighten you most certainly is a criminal offence. They are the ones that could end up in a criminal court.

Even a phone call can be construed as a potentially illegal act. For instance, it could be in a situation that would embarrass you or presumed to have that potential effect.

The consequence of that phone call might be to further jeopardise your financial situation thereby threatening also the arrangement already made.

It is illegal for you to be telephoned at night, say after 9.00 p.m. or before 8.00 a.m. It is illegal for a creditor to contact your family, friends, neighbours or employers.

If you feel that a creditor is harassing, threatening or otherwise making your life miserable then do not hesitate to say so. The law is on your side and you can quickly turn the table on your persecutors by threatening them.

If this doesn't work then do not hesitate to contact your local Trading Standards office. (The threat to do so is usually enough). You will find Trading Standards in the telephone directory under your local authority's services. The Citizens Advice Bureau will also be pleased to sympathise and assure you of your rights.

If you have difficulties in finding information then contact your local authority. They will give you the number to call and the address to call at. Be prepared to visit them and make a formal complaint.

Dealing with Letters, Phone Calls and Personal Visits

How do we deal with that myriad of persecutors? Ignore them? Do we do a runner? Hope they will just get fed up and go away. Threaten them with your heavies? Well, none of these things.

Keep copies of all correspondence, yours, and theirs.

Record all credit-related telephone calls. Do remember though that you should maintain coolness. The object of this exercise is to:

Get evidence of harassment or persecution

Let your persecutor know that he is being recorded
To show you are both determined and astute.

You're nobody's fool.

You may receive a visit at home. This can be distressing and embarrassing to you of course and that is why it is done. Unfortunately, it isn't illegal for them to do so but how it is done could be construed as harassment.

No matter how polite or professional your visitor is it is not wise to allow them into your home.

Talk on the doorstep preferably with your door closed behind you.

They should never call at unreasonable hours; as a guide 9.00 a.m. to 7.00 p.m. is reasonable.

Do point out that you resent the nature of their call and you would prefer contact to be limited to telephone or written procedures. DON'T CALL AGAIN!!!!!! Shut the door.

Should they ignore your advice and call again then the door will either not be opened or slammed in their face. They will be wasting their time

Tell them that you resent their calling on you and give them a reason if you wish. Your mother is ill upstairs, your child is sick, and your employer is visiting you, it could jeopardise your arrangements with your landlady.

Leave them in no doubt that you will be calling in at the Trading Standards office to make a complaint. Ask for his name, business card, and the purpose of the visit and take your visitor's car number. They don't like it when YOU take the harassment initiative.

It is a good idea to have a tape recorder placed near the door. When your visitor calls smile and say you hope he doesn't mind if you record the conversation. It throws them onto their back foot. They don't like it.

Transfer of Assets

Put your home in your wife or partner's name. This is perfectly legal. After all, it is up to you to decide who should benefit from your assets. Your creditors cannot take your home if it belongs to your wife or partner. If you have children, it is better still.

At least a year needs to elapse before your creditors can even consider possessing your home and it is by no means automatic. The important thing to remember is not to leave it until bankruptcy looms. If that kind of difficulty is on the horizon or, even if it could be, put everything you have in the wife or partner's name.

Tips for better budgeting on a tight income and reducing weekly outgoings

Television Licence. The cost of a television licence is quite hefty when you pay it all at once. Pay for it on a monthly direct debit? This way you may hardly notice it.

Television and video rental isn't good budgeting anymore. Whilst creditors appreciate that television/video use is (surprisingly) essential they will look askance at any suggestion that a myriad of expensive channels are essential. Cut out the subscriptions and consider a purchase rather than a rental.

Many local authorities offer grants towards home insulation. This will help to reduce your heating and lighting bills.

Gas and Electricity. Many utilities offer a budget scheme, which spreads your payments and makes it easier for you to budget. Ask about meter installation. If you are on Income Support you can pay for your arrears by Fuel Direct.

Council Tax. Check it out. You might be entitled to Council Tax Benefits, maybe a discount. See also if you can pay in weekly or monthly instalments.

Water rates. Half-yearly invoices can throw a spanner in your budget. Many water companies are happy to accept weekly or monthly payments.

When arranging regular (re-negotiated) payments try to avoid cheque or postal order settlements. They can be expensive.

Most creditors will (if you ask them) let you have a paying-in book or supply of paying-in slips; likewise, a direct debit form. Most banks offer free-standing orders. By these means, you won't be paying bank charges or poundage.

Joint Debts

If two people or more, usually husband/wife or partners have a joint agreement and one falls on hard times then the other person can be pursued for the amount outstanding. Otherwise, you are not responsible for your partner's financial shortcomings. There is an exception to this rule by the way. It is the Council Tax or Community Charge. One partner can't duck out of this one.

Chapter 13
Notes on Council Tax

This is one area of debt (**PRIORITY**) which could land you in a cell so neglect it at your peril. There are payment options of course. See which one suits you.

DEDUCTIONS FROM INCOME SUPPORT: If you are on Income Support your local authority can instruct the Benefits Agency (DSS) to deduct a set amount each week.

Attachment of Earnings

Similarly, if requested by the creditor the Court can attach an order to your employer's salary system. This will deduct a set amount from your earnings that will include salary, overtime, and bonuses.

The money goes to the court and then the court passes it on. Earnings do not include State Pensions.

This method of recovery is rare because it is expensive to the creditor, time-consuming for both and isn't always successful as many debtors are unemployed, unemployable or transient.

Imprisonment

It is thankfully rare that you can be sent to prison. After the distraint procedure, the council can apply to the Magistrates Court for you to be sent to gaol if it should fail.

If you should find yourself in such dire straits contact a local solicitor or your local Citizens Advice Bureau without delay.

Notes on Water Utilities

A rare event is for your water supply to be cut off. Their procedure is the same as that of other creditors so it is important that you contact them and explain the situation quite early on.

Remember that in all situations, not just water, you can ask for and get a private meeting to discuss your affairs.

Try to come to an arrangement (and stick to it) to pay off your arrears that would normally be paid before the next bill falls due.

If that fails, they can issue a County Court Summons against you. If this happens then you will, of course, be obliged not only to pay the arrears but pay for the court charges as well.

Do remember (if you are on Income Support etc.) that arrangements can be made to deduct a set amount. It is worth it to lift the threat of being deprived of this essential.

Electricity and Gas Arrears

These utilities do not need a Court Order to cut you off and they do have the right to do whatever is necessary, including entering your home, to do so. Even if you cannot pay the bill in full start paying a regular amount to reduce it.

Always contact your suppliers to explain your difficulty. Remember they do work to a coveted code of practice and comply (hopefully) with service quality accreditation.

In other words, they are not going to give you a hard time. Always be prepared to ask, in whatever situation, for someone else to deal with your affairs.

Never accept that the person you are dealing with has sole authority over it and you. They do not. If you don't like them or their attitude then say so and ask to be seen by someone else, preferably more senior.

A good but slightly more expensive way of budgeting for gas and electricity is to have a meter installed. It also has the advantage of focusing your mind on the need for minimum use.

These utilities also run budget schemes. These offer staged payment arrangements towards the arrears. These can be fortnightly or monthly.

Hire Purchase

The term Hire Purchase is general and often misunderstood. Everything you buy 'on the drip' isn't necessarily an on-hire purchase. There are all sorts of credit agreements; hire purchase is just one of them. Each type has different rules applied to it. The differences are important so do get copies of original agreements. You know, the ones you never read when you're figuring out how to get that big box out of the shop and into your car.

Creditors can only retrieve the goods if they are on Hire Purchase or Conditional Sale Agreements. In law, you are not the rightful owner until you have made the final payment.

Under all other agreements, you are the legal owner from delivery. The only way your creditors can recover their loss is through the courts for the money, not the goods, owed.

If the goods are under Hire Purchase or Conditional Sale agreements then the company you bought them off can lawfully take the goods back without taking you to court if at the time you have paid less than one-third of the outstanding amount.

If on the other hand, you have paid more than one-third then the goods cannot be repossessed without a court order. Repossessed goods are unlikely to be in a new and re-saleable condition so up to a point we are talking theory here.

Bailiffs

The Council or any creditor can initiate a visit by bailiffs whose job is to take goods (distraint) *the seizure of someone's property to obtain payment of money owed, especially rent.*

Example: *Many faced heavy fines and the distraint of goods that may be sold to cover the debt and court costs associated with it)).*

There is no requirement to allow a bailiff in

Bailiffs cannot force their way into your home unless you have previously let them in so never do so.

* Never sign any papers that they may attempt to hand to you or push through your letterbox. If you do so you may incur extra costs and the bailiffs may then try to enter by force, legally.

If they do enter your home or business premises, they will assess what might be removed for sale. This will exclude rented property, property on hire purchase or on Conditional Sale, or property that can be proved to be someone else's.

Very little household property is worth seizing as it sells at auction for peanuts regardless of what you paid for it. They will, however, use the occasion and the threat of humiliation to attempt to get the owed money from you before they leave! This may be in one or two instalments.

It is interesting to note that it is not the bailiff's job to track you down. The creditor must do this. Hardly surprising therefore that quite often the bailiff arrives to find the debtor has done a runner or there are claims true or false that he or she has done so. If the bailiff cannot find you the ball is back in the creditor's court.

If he hasn't tracked you down within twelve months then the warrant is suspended and he would (unlikely) need to apply for a new one and pay the fee again.

The debtor may apply to the Court to have the warrant suspended if he is negotiating time to pay or is/has been contributing towards the debt.

Try to avoid a bailiff situation. Like prison, it is a last-chance saloon situation. Once they are involved your costs start to rocket and negotiation becomes virtually impossible.

Even if they are involved don't give up on negotiation. More so than ever before this is the time to disarm them by paying something towards the debt. If things are looking desperate and you feel that you are out of your depth contact the Citizens Advice Bureau immediately.

Bailiffs can force their way into business premises.

Did You Know

The establishment benefits from hundreds of millions of pounds unclaimed by those entitled to them. Are you paying too much tax? Are you failing to claim what is rightfully yours?

Tax Rebates

The government's view of the economy could be summed up in a few short phrases: If it moves, tax it. If it keeps moving, regulate it. And if it stops moving, subsidize it. ~ Ronald Reagan (1986).

If you are unsure of your tax status or there have been changes likely to affect it, check your tax code out. This is especially important if you or your partner is not legally married (anymore perhaps); even if you are living with someone.

Professionals are waiting to help you. Contact either your local Inland Revenue Office or Citizens Advice Bureau. They're both in the phone book. They will be pleased to help.

Benefits

Are you claiming all the benefits available to you? You could be entitled to Income Support, Council Tax Benefit, Council Tax Discount, and Family Credit. Advisers are on hand to help you at the Citizens Advice Bureau, the Council Tax Department, and your local Benefits Agency.

Child Support

Mum or dad, if you are separated and still parenting you may be able to obtain child maintenance from your partner through the Child Support Agency.

Family Tax Credit

Even if you are self-employed you are entitled to Family Tax Credit provided that you are not working over 16 hours. A friend of mine picks up over £100 a week from this virtually unknown little additional benefit.

Call in to the appropriate agencies and persistently enquire as to what benefits are available. If you don't ask you don't get. Learn how to screw those who have grown fat by screwing you.

Let your fingers do your walking and your lips do the talking.

Tip

At times it can be difficult knowing who can deal with your particular enquiry or where to find the utility or organisation you wish to contact.

Simply pick up the phone to the Citizens Advice Bureau, Inland Revenue, Trading Standards, Local Authority, Child Benefits Agency, Age Concern, and Job Centre. Although the enquiry may fall outside of their remit you will invariably find them very helpful in pointing you in the right direction. Journalists seem to know a lot. They don't; they just ask a lot of questions and then write the answers down.

Chapter 14
Bankruptcy or a New Stat in Life?

Poetically it is darkest just before dawn. If things are really grim and you don't know where to turn then bankruptcy has to be an option. Because it is the last option people tend to think of it as tantamount to the march to the scaffold.

Let me put your mind at rest. Those who have experienced bankruptcy invariably say two things

1) It was nothing like as bad as I thought it would be.

2) I wish I had done it sooner. With hindsight any regrets? Consensus is I should have done it sooner.

The Cause of Bankruptcy

'The budget should be balanced, the Treasury should be refilled, public debt should be reduced, the arrogance of officialdom should be tempered and controlled, and the assistance to foreign lands should be curtailed lest Rome become bankrupt. People must again learn to work, instead of living on public assistance.' - Cicero, 55 B.C.

I was one of the nine in ten in July 1999. Unable to meet my financial commitments amounting to £60,000, I went through the system and emerged as a bankrupt.

Did I use my last few pennies to drown my sorrows, throw myself into the river, shriek? Like hell I did.

As I carried the burden of failure away on my shoulders it should have been one of the lowest points in my life but it wasn't.

There was a spring in my step, I felt liberated for that is precisely what had happened. I had snapped (for me) the chains of usury. I was no longer a slave to my creditors.

The slate was wiped clean. I didn't owe anyone a penny. This wasn't an ignominious end but a new beginning without burdens. To be honest I did feel anger rising within me but I suppressed it and counted my blessings instead.

Why the anger? After fighting the inevitable all those years, I discovered applying for bankruptcy a lot less painful than I had imagined it to be. Bankruptcy is a lifeboat offered to you. If you are struggling in the water then take it.

For ten long soul-destroying years, I had tried to do the decent thing by paying off my debts. Working it out it appeared I owed about £120,000. Half to the Inland Revenue and the other half to the banking cartels.

They should have thrown themselves in the river. Unfortunately, they did not. Sorry, they went after you instead.

I had worked a seven-day week often till late at night so that I could avoid the humiliation of bankruptcy. What a damned fool I had been.

I remember my wife once saying to me; 'We have paid £70 and it has reduced our debt by £4. You've got to believe it. How would you feel if you handed £70 of your hard-earned to a stranger who without as much as a thank you or kiss my backside handed you £4 in return?

Ironically ~ and there is much irony in the unfolding events, I was no better thought of by my creditors for trying to do the honourable thing. Nobody respects a cow bred solely for milking. For ten long years, I was an indentured slave to Mammon, which I bitterly regret. Still, better late than never.

I also discovered that my debt of £120,000 was small change. Anticipating their demise, less honourable persons than I lived the life of Reilly running up to their liberation via bankruptcy.

They acquired further credit, took out loans, 'purchased' cars, filled their wardrobes with expensive clothes, wined and dined, took holidays and lived life in the fast lane as a passenger in someone else's Cadillac.

The penalties, such as they are, are no more onerous for going out owing £200,000 than for say £20. As the saying goes, some believe you may as well be hanged as a sheep as a lamb.

Chapter 15
Who Do You Owe Mooney To?

'In 2011 the British government was given a disk giving the names of thousands of British tax evaders hiding their money in the HSBC in France.

HMRC Dave Hartnett was appointed to investigate and negotiate a tax deal. Granting HSBC's bankers immunity from prosecution of crimes relating to tax fraud. Seventeen months later he retired and was given a job with HSBC. Chancellor George Osborne refused to prosecute the tax evaders and promptly destroyed the disk, saying that publishing the names was not in the public interest.'

In my case, over 50 per cent of my accumulated debt was owed to the Inland Revenue. Have you seen what the government is spending your taxes on? So, you won't be losing any sleep over the sixty grand they didn't get off me, will you? I didn't either.

As an aside, I can also tell you that the taxman indulged in a little bit of sharp practice to unfairly load my legitimate debt to them. This would have brought them money they were not in any moral sense entitled to.

The taxman is programmed to screw as much money as possible out of us all to make up the shortfall from those who are smart enough to screw him. Morality, common sense, and even legitimacy don't come into it.

Your duty to yourself and your family is to resist. Tax avoidance but not tax evasion is legitimate. Most of the rest of my debts were owed to the banks, financial institutions, and credit card providers.

Now I don't know about you but every time I go into the bank, I raise my hands above my head while they empty my pockets. When it comes to exploitation, they invented the word.

I am not being cynical. We live in rip-off Britain and your government and the financial services sector are heading the pack of baying hounds ripping the clothes from your back. All I did was give them the slip. So do tens of thousands of other people. Do you want me to feel bad about that?

JESSE VENTURA 'You control our world. You've poisoned the air we breathe, contaminated the water we drink, and copyrighted the food we eat. We fight in your wars, die for your causes, and sacrifice our freedoms to protect you.

You've liquidated our savings, destroyed our middle class, and used our tax dollars to bail out your unending greed. We are slaves to your corporations, zombies to your airwaves, servants to your decadence. You've stolen our elections, assassinated our leaders, and abolished our basic rights as human beings.

You own our property, shipped away our jobs, and shredded our unions. You've profited off of disaster, destabilized our currencies, and raised our cost of living.

You've monopolized our freedom, stripped away our education, and have almost extinguished our flame. We are hit, we are bleeding, but we ain't got time to bleed. We will bring the giants to their knees and you will witness our revolution!'

Chapter 16
The Effect on Others

'I hate the use of the word 'vulnerable' to describe people who are more truthfully oppressed.' – Frankie Boyle.

There was a small debt of several thousand pounds owed to a supplier for which I might have had a tinge of regret. 'Sorry mate!'

I rationalised it this way. The supplier, far more streetwise than I was had for years been counter-attacking the system using equally disreputable methods. He had to survive as do millions of others.

Have you any idea of the size of the black economy in this or any other European country? It is so big that even the government backs off from tackling it.

The government call it the informal economy. Any government that even threatened to take a close look at undeclared incomes would be kicked out of office.

I knew that the modest debt owed to my supplier would be artificially inflated and then written off as a legitimate business loss. He would come up smelling of roses.

Why should I feel sorry for him when he was feeling good about the turn of events? The only thing that made him sad was that he had lost a client who had put a lot of money in his till over the years.

The effect on your family

Whether you are self-employed or 'on the books' life ahead is an uncertain road to travel. You never know what is over the horizon. If it were otherwise then there would be no need for lifeboats or lifebelts on ships.

Get rid of your assets. Whatever your circumstances you should always consider the consequence of redundancy or receivership. Few people plan for bankruptcy but that can be a weakness.

I know some very wealthy men who own very little. They live in a house you would kill for but it is owned by their wife or partner.

On a business call, I kept an appointment with an extremely wealthy architect. Damn him, he lived in the most beautiful home in a blue-chip part of Cheshire. Being led inside I gasped with envy as I admired the trappings of his wealth.

Smiling, I told him that our tastes coincided but my income and his didn't do so.

'Michael,' he replied. 'The only difference you and me is that I owe more money than you do.'

Wives and partners are a little more predictable and even if you do fall out, they are more likely to meet you halfway than your creditors will.

Their car/s is likewise owned by someone else, leased, on hire purchase. Whatever, nothing is at risk of repossession or sale to meet outstanding debts.

Have you made a provision? If not don't delay. It is no use trying to unload your home the week before you petition for bankruptcy.

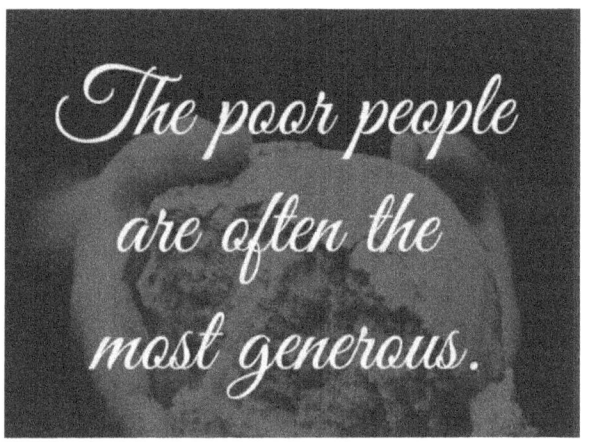

Public Humiliation by Exposure

There is no such thing anymore. The only ones likely to know are those who couldn't care less. By law, a statement of your bankruptcy must appear in The London Gazette and a national or local (usually) newspaper, for example in Merseyside the Liverpool Echo or Manchester the Manchester Evening News. When did you last look at the bankruptcy notices in such newspapers? Does anyone?

Furthermore, the levels of bankruptcy in Britain, where taxes are higher than nearly anywhere else in Europe, are such that you're in lots of good company believe me.

The bottom line is no one knows about your bankruptcy unless you tell them. What effect does bankruptcy have on your lifestyle? I remember chatting informally with an insolvency practitioner. I asked him to what extent it would disrupt my life.

He replied that it isn't normal practice to inform bankrupts after the (normally) three-year period 'of disgrace has been served'.

He smiled: 'You would be surprised how many people call me long after their bankruptcy has expired and restrictions lifted to ask if they are still bankrupt.'

How do I go About It?

The first thing you need to pick up is a copy of 'Guide to Bankruptcy; When, Where, How, Who, What?'

As with anything else I recommend you to pick up such guides are free and you can get a copy from your local Insolvency Service. This is an agency within the Department of Trade and Industry.

You won't find their address in your telephone directories so look up the nearest County Court and ask for the insolvency department.

Simply ask if they have a copy or if they have the address of the local office of The Insolvency Service where you can pick one up. It is an 18-page guide and tells you, in plain English, all about bankruptcy and its effects.

There is no embarrassment. In my local office, there are dozens of copies on hand in the help-yourself racks. While you are there pick up anything else useful. You might also pick up a copy at your local main CAB offices but The Insolvency Service or the insolvency department of your local County Court. There is no point in me repeating too heavily what you will soon have at hand but here are a few points:

Chapter 17
Take a Deep Breath

Can I emphasise that in my experience no one is going to be nasty to you, humiliate or embarrass will you. Everyone is there to help. Go about things with the right attitude. Everyone loves the underdog. I cannot recall a single unpleasant encounter. Except, the from the clerks at my local job centre.

Go to your nearest County Court, and head for the Insolvency Department. Tell the window clerk that you are petitioning for your bankruptcy and need the appropriate papers. No embarrassment and they've heard it all before and are quite matter-of-fact indifferent.

Off you go home again and there you can fill in the paperwork. It isn't difficult. Others can help; local CAB, family or better still your accountant.

You will also find that the lady or gent you are dealing with at the court will help you with any blank spaces you don't understand.

But don't expect them to sit down and do the whole lot with you. In case I forget to mention it afterwards when you do end up with the Official Receiver, he or she will help you through it.

Back we go to the same court and the same window. Don't worry, typically it's all done and dusted within an hour or so of you taking that deep breath and going through the swing doors.

She or he will scan the paperwork and see that it is in order. She will also relieve you of your payment whatever it is now; in 1999 it was £370 sobs. That is the only hard bit.

Ask if there is anything you don't understand. She will then make a same-day appointment for you to put your right hand up in the air and declare your petition to the court counsel or he or she could be a magistrate. In my case, it was come with me and straight up the stairs we go.

It was a simple office, very civil and private. There are only you, the clerk and the magistrate present. Expressionless, he glanced at the paperwork for a few seconds. In my case and hopefully yours too he will ask if there was any particular reason for your financial demise but no details are required.

Answer the question in a sentence. In my case, I simply held my hands up and conceded poor money management on my part.

He smiled, wished me luck, signed the paper and that was it.

Or it was nearly it. As directed, I went to the office of The Insolvency Service with my papers tucked under my arm.

There I met a nice lady practitioner. Sitting down together in a small private office we two went through the paperwork crossing the t's and dotting the i's. It took about thirty minutes and that was it.

I was at this point a self-declared registered bankrupt. She took my chequebook and credit cards so don't forget to take those with you or you will have a second trip.

All credit was stopped at that instant. Now, as I have explained, credit is a burden so why should I feel shock and horror at £120,000 being lifted off my shoulders?

Setting up a Company

Many people who have been declared bankrupt set up a company in their wife or partner's name; it can be anyone reliable and supportive. If you are self-employed, it is your best bet if you haven't already done so.

You will find plenty of registration companies in the business section of periodicals like Exchange & Mart. Prices range from £45 - £150 but they are much of a muchness in terms of what you get.

You can either choose a name that pleases you if it is available or simply register it in the name of an existing vacant company. They are quite easy to set up but your accountant is best doing this and indeed advising you. You will need an accountant anyway.

Once you have registered your company it is technically your wife or partner's business and she now employs you.

She pays you just enough to get by on. As it so happens (coincidentally) your wages will just cover your outgoing.

There is nothing to spare. If on the other hand, there is a little to spare you will be obliged to contribute something of your wages towards the costs of the bankruptcy.

It could be £40 a month but whatever it is a lot less than the sums you would have had to find if you had not so cleverly petitioned for your bankruptcy.

Other Effects

All your debts are dead. You forget them.

Hope you moved your assets (home) otherwise, they will have it especially if there are no children involved. They would make it a little more difficult for them to take it. Oh! Except for a second mortgage. That does have to be paid.

Do not go to an insolvency practitioner. I don't see the point in paying someone to do something easy-peasy and probably better if done by you.

You can be made bankrupt by someone you owe money to (Inland Revenue, Banks, Suppliers, etc.) or you can petition for bankruptcy yourself. What is the difference? As my accountant explained, it is the difference between going into the police station and giving yourself up or waiting for them to come and get you.

The upside to petitioning your bankruptcy is that you decide on the timing. You are not waiting for someone else who may strike when it least suits you. You could, for instance, have just cleared heavy debts just as the blade falls. You have needlessly paid all that money off.

If a major creditor is going to bankrupt you, he will. Don't think that the passage of time diminishes the prospect. The Inland Revenue let me go for seven years before pursuing me for back tax.

Then there was then a year or two of argie-bargy and when we reached the stage where repayment was impossible and bankruptcy inevitable, I waited nine months for them to strike. I don't know when they would have moved because rather than wait, I petitioned for my own. I was in control.

There are a lot of advantages to putting your affairs just as you would like them before having got your timing right, and putting your hands in the air. Also, you are better thought of. The man who gives himself up always is.

The sooner you deal with the problem the sooner you get your sentence completed. If I had taken my own (with hindsight) advice I would have put mine behind me in 1992 rather than 2002.

The downside is that you have saved whoever else might have made you bankrupt £370 (court and administration fees) because that is what it will cost you. Use your overdraft I say tongue in cheek.

It has to be paid by the way, obviously IN CASH. They will not take a cheque or credit card. I wonder why!

Individual Voluntary Arrangement (IVA) might be suggested. Try to avoid it if you can because as far as I can see, whilst it avoids the few restrictions imposed on bankrupts, you still have to repay all your debts.

Bankruptcy theoretically means that the proceeds from your sold assets compensate your creditors. Get rid of your assets well before the chop.

They could take your car for resale if the Official Receiver feels that it is more than is needed to get you around. I JUST managed to keep hold of my Peugeot 405 which was worth £350. Had it been valued at say £1,000 I would have almost certainly lost it.

Bankruptcy proceedings take place in the nearest High Court or County Court to where you live. You cannot pick and choose and there is no point anyway.

An Official Receiver, a civil servant who is usually a specialist solicitor, will be appointed to administer your bankruptcy. They don't bite and they are very helpful. Having said that always be honest and co-operative with them. He/she is paid by the system; presumably your £370.

An Insolvency Practitioner is a legal professional who is best avoided. They will as I say charge you for doing what is incredibly easy yourself.

Unlike County Court Judgement your bankruptcy can be kept on file (Credit Reference Agencies) long after the six years have passed. You will be affected by it.

Life will never be quite the same again so work out alternatives to your old system of gaining credit. It isn't difficult you know and you will be better off without it. You can, of course, request a credit reference agency to record the fact that you are a discharged bankrupt.

Chapter 18
Freedom

Failure is not falling down.
Failure is falling down and refusing to get up again.

Discover Increased Earning Opportunities.

'Attacking the rich is not envy, it is self-defence. The hoarding of wealth is the cause of poverty. The rich aren't just indifferent to poverty; they create and they maintain it' – Jodie Foster.

The sad aspect of modern life is that most people have lost the will or the ability to help themselves. We tend to resign ourselves to the situation we find ourselves in as though it were Fate alone that guided us through life.

When we're down and need to get to our feet again we tend to just give up. But who wants to spend the rest of their life selling Big Issue?

Fate can, of course, deal us hard blows and that perhaps is the reason you are reading this survival guide now. Adversity makes some people weaker, others it makes stronger.

If we avoid failure or rejection, we will almost certainly avoid success as well.

Yes, we are surrounded by inspiration; examples of how people just like us often in far worse situations pulled themselves up and turned failure into success.

Often, they use the experience of failure to get back on their feet. They turn a disadvantage into an opportunity. I am told that statistically successful entrepreneurs were declared bankrupt nine times before they became successful.

Others have entered our world as migrants. They know little and they lack language and communication skills. It is enough for me to say; how do you think you and your family would cope if all of a sudden you found yourselves thrown upon your wits in say Albania or Belgrade?

Going bankrupt isn't the end of the world but the beginning of a new adventure. One man who saw it as such was Florida-based multi-millionaire Vilnis Ezerins. He was one of 1.5 million Americans who go bust each year.

'I knew that going bankrupt wasn't the end,' Says Ezerins whose property empire hit the rocks. 'I started living high and not paying attention to my business,' he says. He declared personal bankruptcy and lost his home, car, and all his savings.

Ezerins moved in with his girlfriend and immediately started another business. He went on to develop an advertising agency and a free newspaper. He is now the president of a multi-million-dollar marketing data business AccuData America.

'There is little difference between people: the little difference is attitude but the big difference is whether it is positive or negative.'

It is all a matter of attitude

If you think you are beaten, you are,
If you think you dare not, you don't,
If you'd like to win but think you can't,
It's almost certain you won't.
Life's battles don't always go,
To the stronger or faster man:
But sooner or later, the man who wins
Is the man who thinks he can.

Who was right? Me or my Neighbour Eddie?

Was I foolish or wise, you decide? Approaching retirement, I fell on hard times. It seemed that fickle fate was dealing me a bad and undeserved hand.

After all, throughout my life, well for 45 years, I had worked, never taken a sickie, paid my taxes, and never claimed a penny off the state. Yes, I boasted about my work principles and my integrity.

Did I get a round of applause? Not from Eddie. My next but one-door neighbour was in his mid-thirties. He boasted that he had never done a day's work.

Eddie lied: I was told that on just one occasion he had been told to work or forfeit his benefits. My neighbour duly turned up and was set to work pruning the local park's trees.

Guess what? Eddie allegedly fell off his ladder and hurt his back. So, Eddie had done maybe a few hours of work in his twenty years of 'working' life.

Eddie, who was as fit as a butcher's dog, preferred to go fishing with his unemployed mates. These fishing excursions were preceded by a few beers in an attractive canal-side inn. By day, Eddie pottered here and there whilst looking after his wife and kids. In truth, Eddie was a first-class family man.

Their lovely home was owned by the local authority and the benefits agency covered all his costs; the rent, utilities, clothing and suchlike for his kids. On benefits, he and his family lived the good life.

And the point? Eddie thought I was dumb for paying into the system he and millions of others – including politicians – were milking.

As I say, you decide who was right. Was I right or was Eddie on the right disused track? HINT: I was the one who went bankrupt and was treated by Social Security clerks as if I were a leper.

My experience with the government departments Social Security and Job Centres reminded my very much of the renowned poem, **It is Christmas Day in the Workhouse** by journalist George Robert Sims. GOOGLE it and weep. There are still today those with hearts of stone, damn them.

The End or the Start of a New Life

BOOKS BY AWARD WINNING MERSEYSIDE WRITER MICHAEL WALSH

RETRIBUTION

A soldier-of-fortune's break in Liverpool sours when he learns that his naive daughter became ensnared by the city's lowlife. This is an epic fail on the part of the traffickers in flesh.

Fraser McLeod is a veteran of the 1960s Congo crisis and Simba Rebellions. When you add the toxic Rhodesian bush wars you're left with a lethal humanoid, a cunning and resourceful predator.

His teenage daughter's trail has gone cold. The action heats up when vengeful MacLeod disappears into the maritime city's social sewers.

Those, whose trade is debt and death, sex and drugs know how to avoid the inquisitive. But they are no match for a prowling marauder for whom death is no more to be feared than is birth.

The soldier-of-fortune turned arms dealer has a single lead and an insatiable thirst for a messy and vengeful nemesis. Based on real life experience the author's account combines the movies Death Wish and The Wild Geese.

Brian Smyth writes, 'An excellent thriller written in the tense style of a John Le Carre spymaster novel'.

'A truly great and gripping story.' adds Anthony Douglas.

Walter Potter comes straight to the point: It is a very exciting and heart-warming story about an ex-mercenary looking for his lost daughter who was being forced into prostitution.

THE STIGMA ENIGMA

Programmed to kill, former mercenary Jack Scarlett is in a no-holds-barred conflict in which no prisoners are taken. Double-crossed in love and trust, in the predator's cross-hairs are the most sinister sinners of Liverpool's underworld.

Determined to stop his high-octane lethal feud is Detective Chief Inspector Eric Jansen. The killer question is, can Detective Chief Inspector Eric Jansen stop Jack Scarlett, and does he want to?

THE SOUL MATES

Paranormal romance challenges your beliefs in the supernatural and pushes the frontiers of morality. Read with closed eyes an open mind, and a readiness to reconsider the morality of romantic relationships. When you reach the last revealing chapter the message on the tombstone will shock. The author places a hex on any who reveal the secret of the tomb. This astonishing novel may well prove to be a revolution in English-Irish literature.

THE DOVETAILS HOTEL AND THE ENIGMA OF TIFFANY

THE DOVETAILS HOTEL and its sequel **THE ENIGMA OF TIFFANY by** Michael Walsh. A tender romantic comedy that focuses on the amorous friendship of Gareth and his attractive lady friends happy to share more than just friendship with the debonair novelist. A reader writes, 'I thoroughly enjoyed it.' There is girl talk, excitement, revelations, dilemmas, compromises, romance, and at times pathos.

GENERAL INTEREST BOOKS

GREAT SAYINGS AND STORIES OF HISTORY

For those searching for inspiration and enlightenment, there are many sources of literature from which to make their choice. Great Sayings and Stories of History go where others dare not go.

The compiler's inspiration finds its genesis in the wisdom of Friedrich Nietzsche: People don't want to hear the truth as they don't want their illusions destroyed.

Those who don't want their illusions destroyed may well be advised to look elsewhere. Great Sayings and Stories of History contain many quotes that will cause them to mutter beneath their breath, 'Well, I didn't know that'.

The volume is not intended to be read as a novel. Pick your copy up whenever you're at a loose end, need something to pass the time with or would like to have your thoughts provoked before you snuggle down for the night.

DEBTOR'S REVENGE

Those who fall victim to the taxman, banks and moneylenders are victims of legalised mugging. The author, who suffered a financial collapse, has put his experiences to good use. **DEBTOR'S REVENGE** teaches you how to turn the tables on your tormentors and rise again from the ashes of despair. Essential Fight-Back Guide for victims of usury, threatening letters, intimidation, bailiffs and bankruptcy.

THE BUSINESS BOOSTER

Of the thousands of business books, why should The Business Booster be exceptional? The author was a top business assessment and recruitment executive for the Guild of Master Craftsmen for twenty years. The expert identified, assessed, recruited and mentored the best of Britain's building and allied tradesmen for the Federation of Master Builders.

Much of the information and advice was based on the advice of the most successful small business owners. The Business Booster is a unique hands-on guide to successfully and efficiently running a small business.

NOTE One reviewer is critical yet the book is a compilation of the best business advice columns that were published over several years in the Euro Weekly News (500,000 readers) and Out and About Magazine Monthly.

'Dear Michael, keep up please those fantastic articles I have no idea how these fascinating stories you bring about. It is incredible how characters come alive in your writing as you read about them and the information is so real. They are so interesting.' ~ Carol Levey, Editor, Out and About Magazine, Spain. (08.02.2021)

RELATED SEAFARING BOOKS

Untold Sagas of the Sea Volume I, II, III and IV

The Leaving of Liverpool

Britannic Waives the Rules

All I Ask is a Tall Ship

by ex-seaman Michael Walsh.

THE LEAVING OF LIVERPOOL

THE LEAVING OF LIVERPOOL ex-Liverpool seaman Michael Walsh, regular television, radio and newspaper personality. Bestseller: 70 stories and over 100 pictures. A first-hand account of the British ships, seafarers, adventures and misadventures (1955 – 1975). A tribute to the ships and seamen of the then-largest merchant marine in history.

BRITANNIC WAIVES THE RULES

BRITANNIC WAIVES THE RULES The last White Star Liner (1845-1960) by Michael Walsh, regular television, radio and newspaper personality. In 68 lavishly illustrated stories the company's last deck boy vividly recalls shipboard life. The liner's colourful characters and jaw-dropping incidents both on board and in New York's notorious Hell's Kitchen. A unique collector's item.

UNTOLD SAGAS OF THE SEA Volume I

Stories of great sea tragedies are often airbrushed or off the radar. The author tells it like it is. A good book makes you want to live in the story. Unknown Sagas of the Sea leaves you no choice.

UNTOLD SAGAS OF THE SEA Volume II

The success of Volume I of the Sagas series inspired demand for Volume II. If your taste is in sea battles and heroic endeavour, submarine warfare, tragedy, folly and daring, you will find Untold Sagas of the Sea Volume II a gripping chronicle of hard-to-believe sea stories we dredged up from the Immortal Seas.

UNTOLD SAGAS OF THE SEA Volume III

The success of Volume I and II of the Sea Saga series stirred interest in reliving (and dying) the most heart-breaking and often avoidable sea tragedies of all time. As your destination might not be as you intend this is not a book to be read before catching a ferry.

UNTOLD SAGAS OF THE SEA Volume IV

Ex-Seaman Michael Walsh keeps the dramas of ships and crews alive. Truth is stranger than fiction as is revealed in nearly 40 amazing seafaring stories we raised from the seabed. A glance at the chapter list will raise your eyebrows and provide you with a lifetime of conversational pieces.

ALL I ASK IS A TALL SHIP

A Liverpool Sailor's Odyssey in pictures and evocative verse. Michael's work in Liverpool alone 3,000 copies of now out-of-print collections cleared the shelves within weeks. Most are here reprinted in earn top revues.

A SEA VENEER OF LIVERPOOL

In evocative multiple beautifully illustrated verses the soul of Liverpool, its history and most importantly the people of Merseyside. Britain and Ireland's most popular living poet – award-winning writer Michael Walsh invariably sells out when he publishes his Liverpool-theme poetry, books and novels.

FORTY SHADES OF VERSE

FORTY SHADES OF VERSE by Michael Walsh in legend, verse and stories provides the enigmatic mirror image of the ancient Irish Nation. The Bard of Ireland's illustrated verse crosses frontiers. The award-winning poet's Irish blood alchemy reveals Ireland's soul, its yearning for peace, love, justice, hope, charity and romance.

MICHAEL WALSH POETRY

Book editions of Michael Walsh collections are beautifully and sumptuously illustrated. Each book features a little over 60 delightful compositions with appropriate images. There are no repeats; the poetry content of each collection is different. These are guaranteed to please you and make the perfect gift.

MICHAEL WALSH POETRY TITLES

A SANCTUARY OF LOVERS

VOICES FROM THE OTHER SIDE

IN LOVE WITH LATVIA

IMMORTAL BELOVED. Michael Walsh.

WHISPERING HOPE. Michael Walsh.

WINE THOUGHTS. Michael Walsh.

A SYMPHONY OF VERSE. Michael Walsh.

HEART TO HEART POETRY. Michael Walsh. Volume I

HEART TO HEART POETRY. Michael Walsh. Volume II

HEART TO HEART POETRY. Michael Walsh. Volume III

FOR THOSE WHO CANNOT SPEAK. (Anti-War Poetry)

FORTY SHADES OF VERSE. (Irish Stories and Poetry)

ALL I ASK IS A TALL SHIP. A Liverpool Sailor's Odyssey.

A SEA VENEER OF LIVERPOOL. The Soul of Liverpool.

YOU TUBE

Michael Walsh's poetry-music has been compiled by noted Italian video impresario, Carlo Gallozzi. Such is the enchantment of these exquisite poetry-video productions that the number of YouTube views quickly surpassed those of household-name recording stars.

The Oldest Love Letter. Poetry by Michael Walsh
The Girl I Met in May. Poetry by Michael Walsh
My Auburn Ma Vourneen. Poetry by Michael Walsh
Ma Vourneen – (My Darling). Poetry by Michael Walsh
How Do We Keep Our Love by Alena Boguslavskaya and Sergey Yakushev, lyrics - Michael Walsh.

Michael Walsh Writing Services

Working from your e-mailed copy I bring your book to retail publishing standards.

Established and amateur writers and authors will find advice, editing and ghost-writing assistance by contacting Michael at keyboardcosmetics@gmail.com

MICHAEL WALSH

Michael Walsh is Britain's most creative and successful multi-topical author.

His refreshingly new perspective book titles enjoy a worldwide following.

Contact Michael Walsh by email: euroman_uk@yahoo.co.uk

Read his stories on his popular website www.michaelwalshwriter.com

www.ingramcontent.com/pod-product-compliance
Lightning Source LLC
Chambersburg PA
CBHW070427180526
45158CB00017B/908